D1728141

RELEASING
the Pain

RELEASING

the *Pain*

The Words of Jesus Christ

Michelle Moreno

XULON PRESS

Xulon Press
2301 Lucien Way #415
Maitland, FL 32751
407.339.4217
www.xulonpress.com

Unless otherwise indicated, Scripture quotations taken from the Holy Bible, New International Version (NIV). Copyright © 1973, 1978, 1984, 2011 by Biblica, Inc.™. Used by permission. All rights reserved.

Printed in the United States of America.

Paperback ISBN-13: 978-1-6628-0355-0
Hardcover ISBN-13: 978-1-6628-0356-7
eBook ISBN-13: 978-1-6628-0357-4

DEDICATION

I WANT TO START BY THANKING GOD FOR everything He has brought me through. This book is in memory of my daddy, Leocadio Torres. I want to thank my children, Chelsea, Scott, and Nicole "Coco" Moreno, who have been through many challenging times with me. As a family, they stood by my side and understood the time I needed to spend with God alone to help me cope with the loss of my daddy and my husband. I would also like to thank my mom and many friends, family, and church family who have become like family!

I also want to thank my ex-husband, Ben Moreno. Regardless of what heartaches he has caused our family, I now understand the cliché saying "hurting people hurt people". Without seeking God to forgive yourself, love yourself, and release all the hurt to the One who can fill that void in our lives, we will continue to walk around lost in this dark, cold world. I am not completely healed, but I thank God I am not where I used to be. I am learning to move forward and to love and forgive my husband for the many times he insulted or rejected his family. I can now love him and those who have done me wrong, because God is LOVE and love covers a multitude of sins...past, present and future.

CONTENTS

Dedication v

Chapter 1 1

Chapter 2 6

Chapter 3 9

Chapter 4 12

Chapter 5 15

Chapter 6 19

Chapter 7 22

Chapter 8 25

Chapter 9 28

Chapter 10 30

Chapter 11 34

Chapter 12 37

Chapter 13 40

Chapter 14 43

Chapter 15 45

Chapter 16 47

Chapter 17 50

Chapter 18 53

Chapter 19 55

Chapter 20 59

Chapter 21 64

Chapter 22 68

Chapter 23 73

Chapter 24 78

Chapter 25 81

Chapter 26 85

Chapter 27 88

Chapter 28 91

Chapter 29 98

Conclusion. 101

CHAPTER 1

HEBREWS 10:36 – "YOU NEED TO PERSEVERE so that when you have done the will of God, you will receive what He has promised."

When I started to write a couple years ago, I did not know I would be writing to publish a book. God knew but, I didn't!

Each day I would spend time reading God's Word and seeking Him to heal my broken heart. My heart was broken into pieces. My daddy, who was my rock, was no longer there to give me Godly advice or wisdom, or to pray for me when I couldn't shake the feeling of sadness from within. Every day I would read a chapter of the Bible, and over time, His words comforted me, gave me the urgency to know more about Him, and the strength to run to Him each time I felt attacked.

This book reflects the things God put in my heart during that season. The Book of Psalms is about praise & worship. The more I read in Psalms, the more I just kept thinking, "This is what I'm going through. This is the solution I've been looking for!" The answers were there all along, I just had to open my Bible and seek out the answers to my questions and problems.

Over the years, I have seen how many people are hurting and how many people have allowed the fear of being rejected by the one they love and the fear of being alone to take root in their heart. People build up walls around their hearts. These walls guard against break-ups. These walls guard against people walking out on them. People tell themselves they won't allow others to take advantage of them again, not realizing all that is doing is hardening their hearts and blocking the appreciation of true love when it comes knocking at their door. They have allowed the hurt from the past to hold them captive.

Many people encounter evil spirits; that voice or thought in your head that tells you, you're not enough; that thought that tells you, you have to repay someone with evil (doing something wrong) for the wrong they have done to you. We have the spirit of "rejection[11]" that says, "I'm going to reject them first, I'm going make them hurt before they can hurt me or turn me down, so I won't get hurt emotionally."

When we can ask God to start healing our broken heart and put together all the shattered pieces, God will start to go to work on us.[12] God will start to make us think, "Is it worth me crying over someone who can't see my worth? If God loves me, why do I fight for the approval of a companion who makes me feel worthless time and time again?" Will it be comfortable? No!

As you continue reading, you may hear concepts or principles discussed more than once. [13] Sometimes God will put things in our heart multiple times [14] to remind us to keep going, to keep being encouraged, and to never give up when trying times come against us . If you make it through one obstacle, you will make it through the next one, and the one after that. Yes, many will come against you, but like it says in 1 Peter 5:10, "And the God of all grace, who called you to His eternal glory in Christ, after you have suffered a little while, will Himself restore you and make you strong, firm and steadfast." God never forgets us. When we allow ourselves to heal properly, as painful as that is, we will be able to forgive and love those who have hurt us the deepest, moving forward into what God has called us to be.

In my life, I have suffered verbal and mental abuse from my ex-husband, but despite the trials and tribulations me and the kids have experienced, our love for him still remains.[15] When we pray for God to deliver us from any bondage that is keeping us captive (alcohol, drugs, resentment, anger, jealousy, fear or whatever we are battling), we need to believe that when we call on God for help, He will help! Not everything we ask in His name will come to pass. We can't pray for something bad to happen to someone who has done us wrong. If we can't pray good for our enemies, let us just pray that God's will be done over our enemies or situation. God is a loving God and a God of justice. Let Him be our vindicator.

A question that should make us stop and really think is, "Do I really trust God?" Our mouth may say that we trust Him, but is our mind and our heart saying, "I don't think He can help me"? Sometimes, we feel like we have to help God and manipulate things to have our prayer requests answered.

He is God! He does not need our help. He created us, so He holds the owner's manual for each of our lives.

How sweet it is to read the words, "Blessed is the one whose sin the LORD does not count against them[16] and in whose spirit is no deceit." in Psalm 32:2. If we really believe with all our heart Jesus Christ has forgiven our sins, when we come to Him, sincerely, asking for forgiveness …[17] we are forgiven!! Now, God does forgive our sins repeatedly, but He wants us to grow in Him and to desire not to sin. John 3:30 – "He must become greater; I must become less."

Sometimes, we can be so vulnerable, carrying the weight of our sins, the stress of our worries, and the concerns for our loved ones. I remember my daddy's words, "God will let you do what you want, but if it's going to a [18] place where we are not supposed to go, He will pull the reins on us." He does that so we won't fall into danger. He's a loving and caring Father who wants the best for us!

CHAPTER 2

WHEN WE SURRENDER OURSELVES TO GOD and have an intimate relationship with Him, we will be able to show a smile that is genuine. When we seek God, things may appear to get worse momentarily, but from time to time, God will give you a glimpse into how He is working on your situation. God wants us to keep our faith. He will not only work on your situation, but work on transforming you into who He has called you to be! Many time's we may think, "I don't need changing, my spouse does!" or "other people have the problem, not me", but that's what the devil has come into this world to do: kill, steal, and destroy (John 10:10). We can pray to become more humble and faithful to Him, even when it seems like God is not being faithful to us and is allowing us to go through the fire, the pain, and the hurt. Remember Psalms 33:4, "For the word of the LORD is right and true; He is faithful in ALL He does"

It is hard to praise God when everything around us is falling apart. How do we praise God when we have a loved one sick, our spouse leaves us, or we wonder how we will provide our families next meal? God will show us! When we praise and worship during these difficulties, we are saying, "God I trust You. When there seems to be no way, You will make a way!" We need to learn to live with "expectancy". EXPECTING for our loved one to be healed, EXPECTING our spouse to come back as a changed person, EXPECTING to have meals for the next day to feed our family. Micah 7:7 says, "But as for me, I watch in hope for the LORD, I wait for God my Savior; my God will hear me." We all have fears; some little, some big. Fears that cause questions like "What will the medical report say? How am I going to pay these bills that keep piling up?" Matthew 7:7 says, "Ask and it will be given to you, seek and you will find; knock and the door will be opened to you."

"The LORD is close to the brokenhearted". Many time's we wonder, "Does anyone care?" We wonder, "Does anyone see the hurt and pain I'm feeling?" We can feel so alone in a world that seems to be passing us by, but when God says He is close to the brokenhearted, we can rest assured

He will put His comforting arms around us. He will still the raging waters inside us that leave us in a frantic, anxious emotional state. You will feel the calmness overcome you. In Psalm 46:10 He says, "Be still, and know that I am God; I will be exalted among the nations, I will be exalted in the earth."

CHAPTER 3

Choosing to follow Jesus is by no means easy. Things can actually get harder once we choose to follow Him. These difficulties can lead many to go back to the "world" and that's what the enemy wants. When the devil sees you are still walking that narrow path[19] (not joining others in a scene of drunkenness, smoking, doing drugs, trying to help others through volunteering at a food bank or etc.) , more fiery darts of deception will come against you. But God says in Ephesians 6:16, "In addition to all this, take up the shield of faith, with which you can extinguish all the flaming arrows of the evil one."

Have you ever wondered why people hate you, when all you have done or shown them is good? Sometimes it's not us they hate, it's something inside of them they don't like. We must not change our character or conform to the image we think others will like. We must be comfortable loving the person God has called us to be. Some may not like the change of confidence, the new found love and respect you have for yourself, but love them anyway and keep moving forward to the destiny He has called out for you. We are put on earth to please our Father in Heaven, not mankind. Sometimes, we want to take matters into our own hands. We try to manipulate things to get the outcome we so desire to see. We must leave it in God's hands. When we don't, we are left tired, stressed, frustrated, and drained from all the "attempts" to change someone or something.

How many times do we wonder how someone evil can get away with doing bad things to others? How can they hurt those who love them causing tears of sadness and confusion, while they are out enjoying life, not caring how their actions affect others? But God clearly tells us not to "fret because of those who are evil" or "be envious of those who do wrong." God says in Ecclesiastes 3:17, "I said to myself, God will bring into judgment both the righteous and the wicked, for there will be a time for every activity, a time to judge every deed." God is a God of Justice. We must not wish evil on the people who do us wrong, but instead release them to the One who does judge. We must pray for their salvation and the repentance of their sins, and that they will accept Jesus Christ in their hearts so they can receive God's Grace and Mercy!

"Keep my tongue from sin" (Psalm 30). That's a hard thing to do. The tongue is a small part of the body, but can cause a lot of damage. If we have no control over the part of our body that can cause so much hurt and division, it will raise chaos wherever we go. James 1:19 says, "My dear brothers and sisters, take note of this: Everyone should be quick to listen, slow to speak and slow to become angry." It's hard to refrain from "defending" ourselves when someone is making false accusations and raising their voices to us. We want to argue our case, even if it ends with words that are hurtful. But God hears all and sees all, He is our Vindicator!

CHAPTER 4

Do you ever feel like you are drowning in sorrow, drowning in deep waters, and crying for someone to help you? Do you ever just fall on your knees and cry to God, with no words to say? Regardless of the unspoken words, God is listening to the tears you shed. He's listening to the unspoken requests that lay heavy on your heart. The more you seek God by reading the Bible, positive Words such as: He will wipe away every tear and He will heal the brokenhearted, will bring you comfort. Listening to worship music lyrics that say, "You are not alone", "I have been redeemed", "when you go through deep waters, and I know that You will be with me" will bring you peace. There are many worship songs that you can just listen to over and over until you start to believe the words being spoken, giving you confidence and faith that "This too shall pass". He will remove all the hurt [110] and replace it with His peace and joy. God will never leave you or abandon you when it seems like everyone has left you. God will protect you and restore what was broken.

We should never try to "get even" with those who do evil to us or speak badly of us. God says in Romans 12:17, "Do not repay anyone evil for evil. Be careful to do what is right in the eyes of everyone." In 1 Thessalonians 5:15 it says, "Make sure that nobody pays back wrong for wrong, but always strive to do what is good for each other and for everyone else." There are many scriptures where God tells us not to repay evil with evil. We can rest assured that God is watching what is done to us, what is being said about us or to us, and He will vindicate us! Our battles belong to Him. What an amazing Father we have! We can rest in His presence and under His protection, knowing we will be okay. This too shall pass.

Have there been times where you have asked, where is God? You read His Word, you pray, you go to church, you worship Him, but yet all you experience is calamity, worry, fear, or persecution? You face distress and disaster, like everything is coming down on you. When you think it couldn't get any worse…it does! But, if we are reading His word, the trials and tribulations should be no surprise to us. He tells us we will face many difficulties, many tests will try our faith, but He sees if we will remain faithful to Him even when it seems He has turned His back on us. He promises to never leave us or forsake us (Hebrews 13:5). So when the enemy wants to bombard us with negative thoughts that say God has abandoned us, that we are all alone, and that no one loves us, remember God's Word and His promises.

CHAPTER 5

Is God worthy of Praise? He most cer-
tainly is!! It's hard to give Him praise, when we're in the
storm, and we feel like He's punishing us. We may ask the
question, "Why is He just sitting there allowing the storm
to come against me?" God loves us, He doesn't bring us
harm. He will allow the devil to do harm against us[111],
only to let it refine us and make us stronger! Like the story
of Job in Job Chapter 1 verse one through twenty-two.
Over time, God will reveal to us why we went through
the trials and tribulations.

Sometimes what we have been praying for will not come
wrapped in the package we thought it would. God will
allow us to walk through fire, but He walks it with us. We
will come out refined, not smelling like smoke! Everyone
makes mistakes, everyone desires forgiveness, but also
mercy. It may hurt us to have to discipline our children,

but there are consequences when they disobey. That's the way Jesus is with us! He loves us enough to correct us when we are disobedient, so we can learn from our mistakes. Romans 12:19 says, "Do not take revenge, my dear friends, but leave room for God's wrath, for it is written: "It is mine to avenge; I will repay," says the LORD."

God loves you no matter what sin you have committed. There is no sin too big to EVER make God stop loving you. People may turn their backs on you and stop loving you, but it's not in God's nature to leave you or forsake (abandon) you. Hebrews 13:5 says, "Keep your lives free from the love of money and be content with what you have, because God has said, "Never will I leave you; never will I forsake you."

Praying for a pure heart doesn't mean you will be perfect. It doesn't mean you will no longer sin or do something God would not do. We must ask ourselves, "If God was to walk with me today[112], physically, in the car, at work, would I do the things I do in secret?" Even though we may hide our pain, hide our sinful acts, and hide the fact that we are not okay from others, we can't hide anything from God. He is always walking with us in Spirit, allowing us to do what we want, but always waiting to hear our cry for help. 1 John 5:15 says, "And if we know that he hears us – whatever we ask – we know that we have what we asked of him."

Psalm 53:1 says, "The fool says in his heart, "There is no God." They are corrupt, and their ways are vile; there is no one who does good." When someone says, "There is no God" it's usually because the sin in their life has completely blinded them from seeing God. Perhaps at one point in their life, they didn't walk with God, but at least they knew God was real. Then, when everything was taken away, they started to build up resentment, anger, and hurt, and their hearts hardened. Little by little, the image of God they once had, started to fade away. So now they feel depressed and alone in the dark, with no one that cares (so it seems). But that's what the devil wants people to believe, so while you're "down on your luck", the enemy is smiling at the plan he created. But John 14:6 says, "Jesus answered, "I am the way and the truth and the life. No one comes to the Father except through me."

When we are trying to walk that right path and seeking after righteousness, obstacle after obstacle, will show up on that path. But when we've been falling prey to the enemy's ways [113] for so long, the devil will do what he can to keep us in bondage. He will wear you out, fighting every good deed, and fighting to keep you distracted! But God has given us the authority to call on Him to help us fight the battles we face on a daily basis.

Jeremiah 33:3 says, "Call to me and I will answer you, and tell you great and unsearchable things you do not know."

Consistency in prayer; consistency in faith. Through each battle we face in life, we have to pray to the One who created us and knows what we are facing and enduring here on earth. Faith may fade when we are attacked by strong enemies, but our God is someone who will clear us of blame and suspicion! We just have to stand strong against all the blows that come against us, trusting God sees all the pain we endure. He won't let evil go unpunished. Isaiah 13:11 says, "I will punish the world for its evil, the wicked for their sins."

CHAPTER 6

PROVERBS 18:24 SAYS, "ONE WHO HAS UNRE-liable friends soon comes to ruin, but there is a friend who sticks closer than a brother."

God knows the friends we need in our lives, to guide us and help us into the destiny God has set before us. But many time's we miss the companionship of past relation-ships that were toxic for us, and we allow ourselves to be pulled back to what doesn't bring us joy. God will remove people from our life so HE can walk us into what He has called for us to do. He can see the future when we cannot. He sees the friends we associated with that would have only led us down a destructive life that God calls us out of.

How many times do we allow ourselves to carry around the hurtful and ugly things someone says out of their own anger? We let those words soak into our hearts, and we think, "Are they really true? Maybe there is something wrong with me". We entertain all those hateful words until they begin to take root in our heart. We have to pray each day for God to put a border of protection around our mind and heart, to protect us from the lies the enemy uses against us that make us doubt who God created us to be. Proverbs 4:23 says, "Above all else, guard your heart, for everything you do flows from it."

[114] God is a God of justice. He sees what people do to us; He hears what people say about us. He sees the unfairness shown to us and the rejection and persecution we experience. Through all the discomfort we experience, we can rest assured that He will deliver justice according to His will. It's not wishing bad on someone, because through the discipline, He will also show mercy. If someone were to keep doing wrong and not pay any consequences; that wouldn't be just. Revelation 3:19 says, "Those whom I love I rebuke and discipline. So be earnest (zealous) and repent."

Proverbs 12:17 says, "An honest witness tells the truth, but a false witness tells lies."

Desperate times...we've all had measures of desperate times. Feeling like we have to do what we have to do to make ends meet. But as I look back, I've said a lot of "I" and "me" during these times. Somewhere along the way, I was leaving God out of providing for me, mentally and physically. I had to change the way I prayed. Instead of, "God I want this or God I need this" I had to start saying, "God I accept whatever Your will is for my life. Help me to be humble and grateful. Let me step out of the way and give You control of my life". Oh, what peace that brought me!! Proverbs 3:5 says, "Trust in the LORD with all your heart and lean not on your own understanding."

CHAPTER 7

How many times have we cried out to God to hear our prayers? Many times, we don't have the words to speak, just the tears that seem to roll down our face, wishing we didn't have to carry all the burdens on our shoulders. But then God speaks, "Come to me, all you who are weary and burdened, and I will give you rest." Matthew 11:28. It may feel like you're being pulled in all different directions, trying to raise your family on your own. God knows about it. We can be at rest, knowing He will provide for us "Our Daily Bread". Psalm 120:1 says, "I call on the LORD in my distress, and He answers me."

Many people delight in speaking lies about others. If we let those lies steal our peace and keep us up late at night worrying about what others think and say, we are giving the enemy power over us. Like it says in verse 4 of Psalms 62, "Surely they intend to topple me from my lofty place;

they take delight in lies. With their mouths they bless, but in their hearts they curse." This is a common thing many have done or experienced at some point in life, but we need God to search our hearts, to reveal to us any area we may be harboring "ugly feelings". Psalm 26:2, "Test me, LORD, and try me, examine my heart and my mind."

Psalm 63:3-4 says, "Because your love is better than life, my lips will glorify you. I will praise you as long as I live, and in your Name I will lift up my hands." Without God we won't ever feel complete. We may seek the joys the world has to offer like alcohol, drugs, sex, shopping, and overeating, trying to fill that void in our life. But in all the things we "try", it only leaves us feeling worse than when we started! We still thirst for that happiness that can only come from Jesus Christ. Psalm 16:11 says, "You make known to me the path of life; you will fill me with joy in your presence, with eternal pleasures at your right hand."

How many times do we find ourselves complaining to our friends, or anyone who will listen? Yet, we still feel like no one understands how we really feel or what we are going through. God understands everything we are going through. He wants us to come to Him and talk to

Him as if we had a friend sitting next to us. He already knows how we feel, but He wants to see our dependency is ALWAYS on Him. John 15:5 says, "I am the vine, you are the branches. If you remain in me and I in you, you will bear much fruit; apart from me you can do nothing." Psalm 145:20 says, "The LORD watches over all who love Him, but all the wicked He will destroy."

CHAPTER 8

Psalm 65:3-4 says, "When we were over-whelmed by sins, you forgave our transgressions. Blessed are those you choose and bring near to live in your courts! We are filled with the good things of your house, of your holy temple." We all have "gifts" that God has given us. We just have to seek Him more so they can be revealed to us. Some are called to preach, some sing, some encourage, some to show compassion, and some to forgive and show kindness, but each gift is different, unique, and special in God's eyes. We should all join together and build up the Body of Christ with each unique talent we have been blessed with.

Psalm 66:10-12 says, "For you, God, tested us; you refined us like silver. You brought us into prison and laid burdens on our backs. You let people ride over our heads; we went through fire and water, but you brought us to a place of abundance." Oh yes!! People can test us for sure, but God will allow us to go through tough times, to break us, to mold us into His masterpiece! He has a calling for each of us, if we continue to walk and trust Him, we will see His hand at work in our life and the lives of others around us. God is a God of the impossible. It may be difficult for us to see, but His plan is greater than what we can see with our human eyes. Luke 1:37 says, "For no word from God will ever fail."

How many are "free" in the world but live in "prison" with emotions like anger, bitterness, unforgiveness, guilt, resentment, and jealousy that keep us captive? All these emotions keep us tied up in bondage, not allowing us to enjoy the freedom Jesus died for us to have. Galatians 5:13 says, "You, my brothers and sisters, were called to be free. But do not use your freedom to indulge the flesh; rather, serve one another humbly in love."

Romans 5:8, "But God demonstrates his own love for us in this: While we were still sinners, Christ died for us."

If we are praying and not seeing any changes, we need to ask God to search our hearts to find out what's hindering our prayers to Him. We don't always want to admit there could be anything wrong with our own actions. Maybe there is some unforgiveness for someone who cheated on you or someone who told lies about you. Maybe there is resentment or jealousy towards someone who got the job you thought you deserved. Whatever it is, may God bring it to the surface so it can be dealt with by Him. We must seek the One who can make us whole again. Heal, let it go, and move on to what God has called you to do. Psalm 147:3 says, "He heals the brokenhearted and binds up their wounds."

We all want to be blessed, but what happens when things are taken from us? What happens when people we love, walk out of our life? Can we still pray and thank God for what He has already blessed us with? Or are we going to grumble and complain that God should not have allowed something in our life, He clearly saw, would cause devastation and destruction? This is where the real test and challenge comes in! Regardless of how many reasons we have to not praise God, we must ask for the grace to praise Him in the midst of any storm. Ephesians 2:8,9 says, "For it is by grace you have been saved, through faith – and this is not from yourselves, it is the gift of God- not by works, so that no one can boast."

CHAPTER 9

THROUGHOUT LIFE, WE SHOULD ALWAYS BE grateful[115]. Like it says in Psalms 106:1, "Praise the LORD. Give thanks to the LORD, for He is good; His love endures forever." We should allow thanks and praise to come out of our lips, instead of gossiping or tearing one another down. When you lose sight of the goodness God has given you, adjust your sights to see what's in front of you and thank Him for the things you have taken for granted. It may not look like at the present time there is something to be grateful for, but there is. The things we overlook, someone else is looking at, wishing they had what we have or could do what we do. That's a reminder for us to always stay humble, help others, and have a thankful and grateful heart, mind and soul.

1 Peter 1:8 says, "Though you have not seen Him, you love Him; and even though you do not see Him now, you

believe in Him and are filled with an inexpressible and glorious joy."

How many times does it feel like we are just drowning in a pool of worry, fear, sadness, loneliness, and grief? God came to save us, to pull us out of the deep pit we are in, and to be our Savior! We are going to encounter feelings of all types, but what we do with those "feelings" is what's important. We can carry all the weight of the world on our shoulders, or choose to lay all our burdens and emotions at the feet of Jesus. Romans 3:23 says, "For all have sinned and fall short of the glory of God."

When we are hated for no reason, we can be reminded that Jesus was hated too. Everything we face here on earth, including the trials and tribulations...Jesus experienced too. He knows what we go through. Following God is not easy. People you thought would never leave, may leave you. They will start to distance themselves from you, because your "interests" are not the same. Perhaps you no longer drink alcohol or "have fun" the way you did before you surrendered your life to Christ. But no matter how many lies the devil tells you, saying you're not loved, you have no friends, or you're alone in the world... rebuke the devil!

CHAPTER 10

Psalm 9:13 says, "LORD, see how my enemies persecute me! Have mercy and lift me up from the gates of death." Romans 8:31 says, "What then shall we say to these things? If God is for us, who can be against us?"

Has there been times you encountered "distress"? Someone you love hurt you, or you received a bad medical report, or lost a job? You cry out to God to hear you in your time of desperation and to take all the hurt away, but it seems like He's not listening and you realize you have to "cry it out". Not only is God hearing our prayers during times of distress, but He's counting the tears that roll down our face. Sometimes the only way to feel His presence and peace is to go through the pain. Romans 8:28 says, "And we know that in all things God works for the good of those who love him, who have been called according to his purpose." Philippians 4:6 says, "Do not be anxious about anything, but in every situation, by prayer and petition, with thanksgiving, present your requests to God."

Hebrews 6:6[116] says, "and who have fallen away, to be brought back to repentance. To their loss they are crucifying the Son of God all over again and subjecting him to public disgrace." At times we may forget what God has brought us through in the past. It may be a different trial you are faced with now, but if God got you through difficulty in the past, He can get you through what you face now. He isn't just the Master at one particular event in your life. He wants to fix all areas, challenges, and hardships that you face in your lifetime and has the ability to do so. God wants control over everything in your life no matter how big or small. He wants to humble you, remove the pride you may be struggling with, and help you with anything you face, now and in the future. Psalm 120:1 says, "I call on the LORD in my distress, and he answers me."

We can't put God to the test by saying things like, "I will believe in You if you heal me from this sickness". We should believe that Jesus died on the Cross and in three days rose from the dead. If God raised Jesus from the grave, what impossibility is there for Him? He can raise a marriage that has died and can open the prison doors of a loved one, so their life is changed and they serve God. We should believe that He can heal us from any sickness and deliver us from anything that is keeping us in bondage. He wants us to believe, even when we don't see anything happening. Not just to believe after the work is done. When we pray with disbelief in our hearts we can end up confessing with our mouths statements like, "oh, it's not going to happen, there is no way". When we do this, we are showing God we doubt His work and we doubt He is big enough to do what is humanly impossible. God doesn't have to prove to us what He is capable of doing for us. He wants our faith to be built up by believing for the things we haven't seen yet. Isaiah 43:18-19 says, "Forget the former things; do not dwell on the past. See, I am doing a new thing! Now it springs up, do you not perceive it? I am making a way in the wilderness and streams in the wasteland."

God is a jealous God. How many times do we go to Him only when it's convenient for us? Are there moments in our life, where friends and family do the same thing to us? They know we are going to help anyone in their time of need, so they abuse our character. They only come to us when they need something. It is frustrating and hurtful when you help and help and they don't seem to appreciate it. This is what we do to God, time and time again. He helps us and delivers us from the pit of despair. We promise to change, but go back to our own sinful ways after we get what we asked for. Is it possible we're showing God we will only call Him when we really need Him, instead of allowing him to be in our daily lives? Or are we showing Him we do not think He is worthy to have our whole body, mind, and soul? In a marriage, a spouse is protective of the love relationship, and desires to fix anything that breaks it or threatens it. God is protective of the love relationship He has with us and rises up against anything that would threaten it. This is the type of jealousy God has for us. This is different than unhealthy jealousy born out of insecurity. He shows us so much LOVE, MERCY, FORGIVENESS, and COMPASSION each day, so that way we don't drift away, worshiping someone or something we make into an "idol".[117]

CHAPTER 11

Isaiah 54:17 says, "No weapon formed against you will prevail, and you will refute every tongue that accuses you. This is the heritage of the servants of the LORD, and this is their vindication from me," declares the LORD.

Generation after generation, we can allow our ancestors "habits" to cripple us in our walk today. We may say things like, "Well, my dad drank all the time, my grandpa drank all the time, so that's what I do, that's where I get it from." Lies! The devil is a liar! He wants to keep us in prison and in a poor mentality, but God has come to help us be overcomers! We should always treat people fairly, not judge them from their "background" or their family history. God is love, and if we are living for God, we should ask the Holy Spirit to intercede and show us how to love like Christ loves us! There will be days when our strength is lacking and we feel weaker than other days. There will be days where we don't want to be kind to others due to our emotional state. We can cry out to God for help and to give us the strength to make it through the day. The enemy is always looking for ways to attack us when we are vulnerable, but God's Word in 1 Peter 5:8 says, "Be alert and of sober mind. Your enemy the devil prowls around like a roaring lion looking for someone to devour."[118] So we can be aware of the devil's schemes to ruin our day before it even starts!

I think we would avoid a lot of the trouble we get ourselves in, if we would seek God and ask for His direction on how we are supposed to handle things. Is there something we are making a "god" in our life? Something of more importance than the One who gives us breath each morning when we wake up? Having another "god" in our life is not just a statue. It's something we worship or place in higher importance over Him (our spouse, money, job, alcohol, phones, even food). God speaks to us in different ways, trying to get our attention, but we can be stubborn and do our own thing. He will allow us to keep doing what is pleasing to our flesh and be there when things fall apart. That is His grace and mercy! Matthew 6:24

says, "No one can serve two masters. Either you will hate the one and love the other, or you will be devoted to the one and despise the other. You cannot serve both God and money."

2 Thessalonians 3:3 says, "But the LORD is faithful, and he will strengthen you and protect you from the evil one."

Sometimes you have to fall hard on your face for you to be able to look up to the One who can help you. We all have demons, some visually, some that are struggles and strongholds of hurt, bitterness and unforgiveness, that try to keep us in prison[119], but only God can break those chains that are weighing us down. John 8:36 says, "So if the Son sets you free, you will be free indeed."

CHAPTER 12

JEREMIAH 29:12-13 SAYS, "THEN YOU WILL call on me and come and pray to me, and I will listen to you. You will seek me and find me when you seek me with all your heart."

If God withheld His love and mercy from us, [120] we would be in bad shape. What an amazing God we serve, that when we make a mistake, He does not put a "mark" next to our name, the way we "mark" those who hurt us or do us wrong. When we "mark" others, little by little, we pick up bricks of anger, jealousy, bitterness, and resentment, not realizing it's only weighing us down. Others may throw insults at us, but that is often how they are coping with the issues they are battling. Psalm 23:2 says, "He makes me lie down in green pastures, He leads me beside quiet waters."

There is nothing or no one who can bring us happiness [121] like God can. Like Galatians 5:22 & 23 says, "But the fruit of the Spirit is love, joy, peace, forbearance, kindness, goodness, faithfulness, 23 gentleness and self-control. Against such things there is no law." Things may bring "temporary" happiness, but eventually it will run out. Isaiah 43:1-2 says, "But now, this is what the LORD says - he who created you, Jacob, he who formed you, Israel; "Do not fear, for I have redeemed you; I have summoned you by name; you are mine. When you pass through the waters, I will be with you; and when you pass through the rivers, they will not sweep over you. When you walk through the fire, you will not be burned; the flames will not set you ablaze."

2 Timothy 2:13 says, "If we are faithless, He remains faithful, for He cannot disown Himself."

There is no one like God! Others may try to "play god" like their words are of significance and we should take them to heart. But God warns us to be aware of false prophecies. The "words" that Jesus spoke are the words written in red, found in the Bible, but God also spoke through many authors inspired by the Holy Spirit to bring us so many words of comfort, healing, peace and enjoyment. [122] Those precious words are what we should read and meditate on to bring about guidance and wisdom, and to seek His direction and correction in our life. Psalm 143:8 says, "Let the morning bring me word of your unfailing love, for I have put my trust in you. Show me the way I should go, for to you I entrust my life."

CHAPTER 13

2 CORINTHIANS 11:3 SAYS, "BUT I AM afraid that just as Eve was deceived by the serpent's cunning, your minds may somehow be led astray from your sincere and pure devotion to Christ." Do you ever feel like you have failed as a parent? That even with all the praying, taking them to church, and teaching them about God, they chose to go down the wrong path that you know will lead to destruction. You tried to teach them right from wrong, but they were influenced by their peers. We can relate this to, how many times does God speak to us, to teach us right from wrong. But yet, we want to have fun and not deal with the difficulties that are presented to us in the "now" moments in our life. Just like a parent does not stop loving their child when they choose the wrong path, God says He won't take back His love from us even if we become disobedient and drift away from Him. Isaiah 49:15 says, "Can a mother forget the baby at

her breast and have no compassion on the child she has borne? Though she may forget, I will not forget you!"

Have you ever wondered how long someone will continue to live in sin even though it leads to trouble? We can pray and pray for our loved ones who have found themselves living a destructive, tormented life while not wanting help or to change their sinful ways. We can worry about what happens if they never change their life and God comes back and they go to hell. This scripture in 2 Peter 3:8 says it all, "But do not forget this one thing, dear friends: With the LORD a day is like a thousand years, and a thousand years are like a day." God doesn't want anyone to perish but to have life in abundance! If we have been praying and praying, and no changes are seen, we continue trusting in Him. God will change the heart of the roughest, toughest person you would never imagine being changed. But that's how big our God is. He does the impossible. Ezekiel 36:26 says, "I will give you a new heart and put a new spirit in you; I will remove from you your heart of stone and give you a heart of flesh."

Whenever we find ourselves lost in the wilderness, with no sense of direction, anxiety, fear, and worry can start to creep into our minds. But in the midst of all that darkness surrounding us, there is a spot of light drawing us near. God is near to those who call for help. He is our place of safety. No matter what seems to be closing in around us, He will keep us safe. Psalm 32:10 says, "Many are the woes of the wicked, but the LORD's unfailing love surrounds the one who trusts in him." 1 Thessalonians 5:16-18 says, "Rejoice always, pray continually, give thanks in all circumstances; for this is God's will for you in Christ Jesus."

God's Word never goes "out-of-date". He does not lie. He doesn't break a promise. When we find ourselves gossiping, or telling a "little white lie", who will notice? God will! We should not pretend to be one way to people who are watching and then behind closed doors remove the mask showing who we truly are, someone filled with hurt, anger, bitterness, jealousy, worry, and fear. God knows our true identity. There is no "show" we have to perform for Him to love and accept us, He loves us just the way we are. 1 John 4:16 says, "And so we know and rely on the love God has for us. God is love. Whoever lives in love lives in God, and God in them."

CHAPTER 14

Discipline is a good thing. Haven't you ever disciplined a child to teach them right from wrong? Our Father in heaven will discipline us, not because He is mad and wants to punish us, but because He loves us. He doesn't want to see our lives end in destruction. The LORD will give us relief from the troubles we face; meanwhile the devil gives temporary pleasure only for it to lead to torment. This leaves you vulnerable and trapped in the repetitive sin that keeps you in prison. Some may get away with their sin/crime here on earth, but God promises to repay people for their sins if they choose not to repent. Hebrews 12:6 says, "Because the LORD disciplines the one He loves, and He chastens everyone He accepts as his son."

Our hearts can become hardened, leaving no room to receive the love God has for us. That one person we poured so much love, time and effort into, has now left, leaving a void in our life that is now being filled with inse- curity, anger, resentment, bitterness, worthlessness, and the inability to trust anyone! But God wants to fill that void with His love, peace, joy, worth, value, mercy and grace. He wants to give you back a heart to receive the love and joy He desires you to have. True happiness can't come from a man or a woman, possessions or wealth. It can only come from God! Psalm 16:11 says, "You make known to me the path of life; you will fill me with joy in your presence, with eternal pleasures at your right hand."

Colossians 1:10 says, "So that you may live a life worthy of the LORD and please Him in every way: bearing fruit in every good work, growing in the knowledge of God."

CHAPTER 15

IN THE END, THERE WILL ONLY BE ONE TO reign over this world. There will only be one God people will bow down to. All the idols and gods we worshipped here on earth will come to ruin. May we remember to praise His Holy Name, Jesus Christ, the One who died on the cross and sacrificed His life, so we wouldn't have to pay the price for OUR sins. What a sacrifice and true love! Deuteronomy 32:39 says, "See now that I myself am he! There is no god besides me. I put to death and I bring to life, I have wounded and I will heal, and no one can deliver out of my hand." 2 Thessalonians 1:6-8 says, "God is just: He will pay back trouble to those who trouble you and give relief to you who are troubled, and to us as well. This will happen when the LORD Jesus is revealed from Heaven in blazing fire with His powerful angels. He will punish those who do not know God and do not obey the gospel of our LORD Jesus."

Do you believe God is real? Do you believe He listens when you pray or cry out to Him? Sometimes God is not listening to the words we speak, but to our hearts. Are our hearts lining up with the words we pray? Are we praying for a loved one, praying for a change in ourselves, while our heart is really sending doubt to our mind? Are we asking God to change us, while our heart still wants to do things we know wouldn't be pleasing to God? As painful as it may be, we must first ask God to search our hearts and reveal to us any area we must work on. Psalm 139:23,24 says, "Search me, God, and know my heart; test me and know my anxious thoughts. See if there is any offensive way in me, and lead me in the way everlasting."

CHAPTER 16

KNOW THAT THE LORD IS GOOD. Just to meditate on those words can bring such comfort, knowing the Father we serve, will ALWAYS have our back! You can't put the LORD in a location or a shrine to worship. God is everywhere. He is with us. That's where the enemy tricks us. The enemy can cause us to think we have to search to find this "holy place", but God's power is within us, if we believe! Matthew 22:29 says, "Jesus replied, "You are in error because you do not know the Scripture or the power of God."

1 Timothy 4:4 says, "For everything God created is good, and nothing is to be rejected if it is received with thanksgiving." Once God comes into your life, the things you were once comfortable doing with your friends, will become "uncomfortable", and doing the things you know are not pleasing to God, will become unpleasant. The

things you did "in secret", you no longer feel right doing because you care about the One who is with you. You will no longer be disturbed by what others say and think about you, or what you did. You will want to live the life that aligns with God's Word. Are we going to get it correct? Absolutely not! Are we going to continue to sin? Oh yes! But the more we seek God and follow Him and His footsteps, the more we become like Him. This is just like when our children look up to us (we lead by example) and do what "mommy or daddy does". Romans 12:2 says, "Do not conform to the pattern of this world, but be transformed by the renewing of your mind. Then you will be able to test and approve what God's will is - His good, pleasing and perfect will."

2 Corinthians 4:8,9 says, "We are hard pressed on every side, but not crushed; perplexed, but not in despair; 9 persecuted, but not abandoned; struck down, but not destroyed." Do you find yourself praying for your spouse, children, family, and friends, yet you forget to pray for yourself? It's not selfish to pray for yourself. It's by prayer and petition that you can become that loving and compassionate person God desires you to be. We must continue to ask God to help us walk through this journey and

thank Him that He's walking it with us. Has there been times you've been so broken and tired from a broken heart or an illness, that you don't eat, or even have the energy to get out of bed? Psalm 9:9 says, "The LORD is a refuge for the oppressed, a stronghold in times of trouble."

Has there been times you felt isolated and all alone, with no one by your side? Has there been times you have been looking around for someone to notice you, someone to reach out and lend a hand, or a shoulder to cry on? Has there been times when seeing your weakness, your enemies seem to taunt (mess with) you even more? Has there been times with many sleepless nights and days without eating, not realizing you were making yourself even weaker? No one notices the tears we shed behind closed doors. Sometimes we seem to pray to a God that doesn't seem to be answering our prayers. But don't lose faith, God is listening!! He loves you, He won't let you go through that heartache or sickness alone. He is right there suffering with you. 1 Peter 5:10 says, "And the God of all grace, who called you to His eternal glory in Christ, after you have suffered a little while, will Himself restore you and make you strong, firm and steadfast."

CHAPTER 17

PEOPLE CHANGE: SOME FOR THE BEST AND some for the worst. Some people may change from one personality one day, and the next day show a completely opposite personality. But God's character, His love, His ways, and His promises, never change!! God doesn't love us one day and hate us the next. God loves us, even when we are unlovable. No matter how many times we push Him away, no matter how many times we feel like we don't need Him anymore. He's always standing by, waiting for that moment when we do call on Him for help. He holds no grudges. He is a loving, forgiving, merciful Father, and there is no one like Him. Hebrews 13:8 says, "Jesus Christ is the same yesterday and today and forever."

Revelation 4:11 says, "You are worthy, our LORD and God, to receive glory and honor and power, for you created all things, and by your will they were created and have their being." God will continue to show us just how amazing He is!! Have you held on to a grudge for so long that you can't remember any of the good memories you once had with that person? Is it hard to forgive and forget? Yes it is, but we can replace those thoughts with the thought of how many times we have disappointed God, yet He still shows us love and compassion when we truly call on Him in our time of need. That will slowly melt our hearts to forgive. You may not be able to easily forget, but at least you're no longer letting your heart be hardened from past mistakes and hurts done to you. You will feel joy inside of you that you can't help share with others!! Ephesians 4:32 says, "Be kind and compassionate to one another, forgiving each other, just as in Christ God forgave you."

We should be very thankful that God doesn't treat us based on the sins we commit. Sometimes we compare sins by saying things like, "Well I don't steal, I don't cheat, I don't hurt anyone, so I'm not sinning." But do you have hate towards someone who did cheat on you or stole from you? God says in 1 John 3:15, "Anyone who hates a brother or sister is a murderer, and you know that no murderer has eternal life residing in him." Ask God with a sincere heart to help you forgive the unforgivable because that same grace He shows you, you have to show it to others. Just like a loving parent is happy to help their child when they ask for help, God is there to help when we ask. Colossians 3:13 says, "Bear with each other and forgive one another if any of you has a grievance against someone. Forgive as the LORD forgave you."

CHAPTER 18

PSALM 111:10 SAYS, "THE FEAR OF THE LORD is the beginning of wisdom; all who follow his percepts have good understanding. To him belongs eternal praise." Having fear of our Father in Heaven[123] , is not the same fear you would probably think. It's the kind of fear a child or young adult would have for their parents if they disobeyed their rules. It's not so much the punishment they would get from their parents, it's the disappointment on their face that would hurt worse than a spanking! Well that's the kind of fear God wants us to have with Him; that we want to be obedient to Him in all areas as to not disappoint our Father; to follow His Commandments. Proverbs 8:13 says, "To fear the LORD is to hate evil; I hate pride and arrogance, evil behavior and perverse speech."

Romans 13:2 says, "Consequently, whoever rebels against the authority is rebelling against what God has instituted, and those who do so will bring judgment on themselves."

Matthew 17:20 says, "He replied, "Because you have so little faith. Truly I tell you, if you have faith as small as a mustard seed, you can say to this mountain, 'Move from here to there,' and it will move. Nothing will be impossible for you."

CHAPTER 19

Isaiah 43:2 says, "When you pass through the waters, I will be with you; and when you pass through the rivers, they will not sweep over you. When you walk through the fire, you will not be burned; the flames will not set you ablaze."

God is ALWAYS good. Even when we can't see any goodness in our lives, He's giving us a good thing to be thankful for. We just have to dig deep, past the sorrow we are feeling, past the unworthiness we may be feeling. We can't compare our lives with someone else's life. Each person has trials they face, maybe not in the same moment as you, but they have experienced a "season" of difficulties. Just like we have fall, spring, winter, and summer, we know change will happen; we just have to keep pressing forward waiting for whatever season comes next. You will make it through!

Philippians 2:3 says, "Do nothing out of selfish ambition or vain conceit. Rather, in humility value others above yourselves, not looking to your own interests but each of you to the interests of the others."

We all want recognition for what we do or accomplish in life, but who we seek it from is very important. If we seek the "approval" of human beings, we can get disappointed in life. It's no one else's job to encourage you, to make you feel "worthy" or "valuable". The more you seek God and know who He has called you to be, the more you will start walking around with a confidence that can only be given by our Father in Heaven! 1 Thessalonians 2:4 says, "On the contrary, we speak as those approved by God to be entrusted with the gospel. We are not trying to please people but God, who tests our hearts."

No one is "too far gone" for God to save them. Our faith should increase, not decrease when we don't see changes. We are showing God that despite not seeing our prayers immediately answered, we are living with expectancy! How many times do we just want to take care of and love someone, but each time it feels like they don't want our help or recognize we are just trying to help? God wants to take care of us and protect us from the life that can harm us, but we often choose to "ignore" His love and guidance and do our own thing. When we do this, He will let us do what we want and watch us as we go through trials but He is still with us. The enemy comes to show us a life full of glamour, fun, and reckless behavior, but it all ends up being torment. 1 John 3:8 says, "The one who does what is sinful is of the devil, because the devil has been sinning from the beginning. The reason the Son of God appeared was to destroy the devil's work."

Many time's in the Bible, God says He will "deliver us". Many time's God has rescued us from a pit we dug ourselves, just to watch us end up back in the same hole. Time after time, God will deliver us when we cry out to Him, but God wants us to surrender to Him so we do not fall back into the temptation of sinning against His word. We can get tired of doing the same thing over and over, repeating the cycle of abuse that has kept us captive for so long, but feel like we have nowhere to turn. God is the escape route! No matter how many times we rebel against God and take His love and help for granted, He remembers the covenant (agreement) He made with us, and because He loves us so much, He welcomes us with open arms each time! Isaiah 30:18 says, "Yet the LORD longs to be gracious to you; therefore He will rise up to show you compassion. For the LORD is a God of justice. Blessed are all who wait for Him!"

CHAPTER 20

PROVERBS 22:6 SAYS, "START CHILDREN OFF on the way they should go, and even when they are old they will not turn from it."

If we are struggling, and trouble seems to find us at every corner, we should step back and examine our ways. It's not the fault of our parents or others, it's the rebellion we choose to live. It's hard to walk that narrow path; not many choose the narrow road. Sometimes we may walk alone, and sadness may overcome us, but remember, God is near, walking next to you. Don't let go of His hand and wander off. God always hears the cries of His children, no matter how long it's been since we've prayed or gone to church. He doesn't have regulations on when and where to call unto Him. He wants you to surrender yourself, humble yourself, and ask Him into your heart to help you. Matthew 28:20 says, "and teaching them to obey everything I have commanded you. And surely I am with you always, to the very end of the age."

Proverbs 3:5 says, "Trust in the LORD with all your heart and lean not on your own understanding."

God gives strength to the weak, comfort to the hurting, and love to the orphans. It can seem like one person is against you, then another, then more, until it seems like an army is coming against you! You have the most powerful "army" behind you…God! He's holding you up against anything and anyone that is trying to come against you. "With God we will gain the victory" 2 Corinthians 12:10 says, "That is why, for Christ's sake, I delight in weaknesses, in insults, in hardships, in persecutions, in difficulties. For when I am weak, then I am strong."

Have you ever had people lie about you, making it so "believable" that others who hear these lies are convinced they are true? You even believe the lies at times!! But deep down you know the truth, because God lives in you. He is the way, the truth, and the life! God hears everything that is being said about you. It's not our place to try and defend ourselves, you are a child of God!! Once you know who you are in Him, (worthy, beautiful, strong, smart, loving) all those other "lies" won't matter!! Matthew 5:14 says, "You are the light of the world. A town built on a hill cannot be hidden."

"If looks could kill, if words could kill." Praise God those statements are not true! But words can kill part of our spirit, if we allow it. Words can be hurtful, and words can bring us down to a state of not knowing what or who we are anymore. You can be the kindest person and people can still find a reason not to like you or even a reason to hate you. Don't let that change the person God wants you to be; don't let anyone change your character. Continue to love life, love people and most of all, love yourself! 1 Peter 3:9 says, "Do not repay evil with evil or insult with insult. On the contrary, repay evil with blessing, because to this you were called so that you may inherit a blessing."

Numbers 23:19 says, "God is not human, that He should lie, not a human being, that He should change his mind. Does he speak and then not act? Does he promise and not fulfill?"

When others speak of the "wonders" God has done in their lives, it gives us hope that it's possible for change to happen in our own life. It boosts our prayer communication! I've heard of various testimonies where families struggled with someone they loved on drugs, violence, homelessness, and God came in the nick of time, and saved their family. God is a God of restoration! Many people are feeling so lost, dealing with depression, loneliness, feeling like no-one understands what they are going through, but the more we get into our Bibles, the more TRUTH is revealed to us about the things we are faced with. 2 Timothy 3:12 says, "In fact, everyone who wants to live a godly life in Christ Jesus will be persecuted," Many will try to get a reaction from you, to get you angry, to steal your peace, to accuse you of wrongdoings, but if we can go and speak of "gossip" or "drama", stirring up conflict wherever we go, why can't we use our voice to bring peace and hope to others?[124] Ephesians 4:29 says, "Do not let any unwholesome talk come out of your mouths, but only what is helpful for building others up according to their needs, that it may benefit those who listen."

Galatians 5:22,23 says, "But the fruit of the Spirit is love, joy, peace, forbearance, kindness, goodness, faithfulness, gentleness and self-control. Against such things there is no law."

If we don't start with ourselves, how are we to lead our children the way God wants us to go? Everything we own does not belong to us. You may think, "I'm the one who works hard for everything I have, how does it not belong to me?!" Whether old or young, God gives us the strength and ability to "work hard" for the things we have. God wants to bless us abundantly, but not at the cost of us forgetting about Him. When we have everything we desire...the job, the relationship, the wealth, the fame...He wants to be the only One we "worship". He wants to be FIRST in our lives. Matthew 6:33 says, "But seek first His kingdom and His righteousness, and all these things will be given to you as well."

No one is above anyone else. We all have flaws. No one is perfect. We were created in God's perfect image, but we have some "kinks". God knew that, but He wanted to be sought by us. [125] We all need a Savior. If we as parents taught our kids everything there is to know about life (figuratively speaking) and our kids said they didn't need us anymore, we would feel sad knowing we are not needed anymore. We all want to feel "needed" or "wanted". God's love is unconditional. He loves us no matter how many times we may turn our backs on Him, His love doesn't come with regulations, He takes us all broken and worn out. [126]

CHAPTER 21

1 Thessalonians 5:21-22 says, "but test them all; hold on to what is good, reject every kind of evil."

God is a God of restoration. He just wants us to believe He can do the impossible. May our words and prayers align with what God's word says. May we speak of His goodness with others. Your sickness...HEALED! Your family...RESTORED! Your finances...BLESSED IN ABUNDANCE!! Mark 9:23 says, "If you can?" said Jesus. "Everything is possible for one who believes."

Ephesians 5:5-7 says, "For this you can be sure: No immoral, impure or greedy person - such a person is an idolater - has any inheritance in the kingdom of Christ and of God. Let no one deceive you with empty words, for because of such things God's wrath comes on those who are disobedient. Therefore do not be partners with them."

"The LORD remembers us". Many time's we may feel like God has deserted us. We may ask questions. "Why did He leave me to endure this suffering? Why am I going through this horrible sickness? Why is the hurt from this break-up not leaving me?" We become vulnerable when we are hit with a difficulty that leaves us feeling helpless. With nowhere to run, we want to escape the moment we're in! As much as it hurts God to see us in such pain, He smiles because He knows the final outcome! He knows the tribulation we face now will only teach us, make us stronger, make us wiser, and make us more dependent on Him. Nahum 1:7 says, "The LORD is good, a refuge in times of trouble. He cares for those who trust in Him."

I love God, "For He heard my voice". But what happens when it seems like He doesn't hear our voice? The devil is sneaky and with any little "crack in the door" he will quickly push himself inside, filling our heads with doubt, temptation, and lies. "Why doesn't God hear me? He sees me crying and He still does nothing to take away the pain!". We then start to wonder if God can really do what He says. Will He deliver us from the pain and ridicule? Yes! God never breaks a promise. If He says it, He will deliver it! People will tell you, "Oh, you will be okay, you will get through this". But do we really believe that? The pain from our past seems to haunt us, the present pain seems to dig itself deeper and deeper, feeling like it will never end. But God's word can bring us so much comfort if we turn to Him and read the important word's He has for us to bring healing, to bring comfort, and to bring peace!

2 Timothy 3:16 says, "All scripture is God-breathed and is useful for teaching, rebuking, correcting and training in righteousness."

We can become so tangled up in the emotions that we're feeling that we leave no room to feel God's presence. When this happens, we back ourselves into a dark place, crying for God to help us. Asking Him to remove the hurt we are feeling and wanting it all to disappear. But God can reach all the way down into the pit we have dug ourselves into, that has left us feeling like the world is caving in on us! God loves you too much to keep you in the place you made for yourself. Romans 5:8 says, "But God demonstrates his own love for us in this: While we were still sinners, Christ died for us."

John 14:6 Says, "Jesus answered, "I am the way, and the truth, and the life. No one comes to the Father except through me."

CHAPTER 22

A LOVE THAT LASTS FOREVER, WE ALL WANT that. We seek for humans to give us "true love" that can only be given by the One who created us. He wants us to have a love relationship with us; to fulfill the desires we long for...security, companionship, and happiness. We get caught up believing the lie of the devil that "there's no such thing, there's not a perfect person that gives you everything you want". That's true. There is no "perfect person" or "perfect relationship". But, when two people decide they will follow Jesus together and face the trials, temptations, and tribulations that come against them in prayer, that makes it perfect! When you first seek the perfect One, He will work on your behalf to bring into your life the man or woman who is right for you and who is also seeking Him first. That relationship can be built on both people having fear and love for the LORD! Matthew 6:33 – But seek first his kingdom and his righteousness, and all these things will be given to you as well. Amen!

1 Peter 5:8-9 says, "Be alert and of sober mind. Your enemy the devil prowls around like a roaring lion looking for someone to devour. Resist him, standing firm in the faith, because you know that the family of believers throughout the world is undergoing the same kind of sufferings."

Philippians 4:6 says, "Do not be anxious about anything, but in every situation, by prayer and petition, with thanksgiving, present your requests to God."

In a world that has become more evil with sex, drugs and violence, it seems to be part of "popularity" a "common thing" to participate in these things. But standing alone to obey God's word is better than following the crowd. It's not just young people who suffer with the sexual temptation, it's older people as well. The devil doesn't care if you're single or have been married over 30 years! He will use any tactic he can to cause strife (arguments) and division in marriages, friendships, and families. John 10:10 says, "The thief comes only to steal, kill and destroy; I have come that they may have life, and have it to the full."

There is nothing we can keep hidden from God. There may be things we are ashamed of that we don't want others to know, but we have to be honest with Him and give an account of the actions and feelings we are having that no one else knows about. Sometimes we get so good at concealing our true emotions that people may think we are okay, but we've suppressed so much hurt, anger and hate down in our souls that we are dying inside! Every morning we wake up and decide we will put on our "mask" for the day and pretend we are happy. We think, "If I don't think about it, it won't ruin my morning." False! The devil is good at lying to us. [127] God wants to remove EVERY TROUBLING THING that you have decided on your own that you are going to continue living with. Without Christ moving into your heart, are you truly "living" or "just getting by"? Galatians 1:10 says, "Am I now trying to win the approval of human beings, or of God? Or am I trying to please people? If I were still trying to please people, I would not be a servant of Christ."

Psalm 119:33,34 says, "Teach me, LORD, the way of your decrees, that I may follow it to the end. Give me understanding, so that I may keep your law and obey it with all my heart." What a wonderful Teacher we have! We have the opportunity to genuinely search Him and the happiness that can come from following Him. Does it mean we will experience joy all the time? Absolutely not! But are we just seeking God for a short time, just to get something in return? Or do we really want to have that relationship with Him and receive nothing in return? What if we don't get that job we've been praying for? What about that spouse that we've been praying for, the one who will respect and treat us right, or what about the healing of yourself, your child, or another loved one? What the "world" has to offer is worthless compared to the treasures we are storing up in heaven! We shouldn't take God's word lightly. He wants to give us the desires of our heart, but not if it's going to lead us to destruction and take the place of His existence in your heart. Hebrews 11:6 say, "And without faith it is impossible to please God, because anyone who comes to him must believe that he exists and that he rewards those who earnestly seek him."

Romans 8:28 says, "And we know that in all things God works for the good of those who love him, who have been called according to his purpose."

What are God's commands? I think we've all heard, read, or seen pictures of the Ten Commandments. But His commands go deeper than that. His instruction is to help us live a life of peace, joy, and contentment resulting in a desire for more of God and not worldly things. We should reflect back on our way of living and ask "does that really bring me happiness?" Psalm 119:1-3 says, "Blessed are those whose ways are blameless, who walk according to the law of the LORD. Blessed are those who keep his statutes and seek him with all their heart - they do no wrong but follow his ways."

It's easy to forget about God's laws when someone is being mean and ugly towards us and all we want is to be mean back. Or when someone says untrue things (lies and rumors) about us and we want to tell lies about them to hurt them. But that's how the devil fights his battles, with retaliation! We must ask God to teach us His ways, to bring about peace in all circumstances. If we fight every time someone looks at us wrong or lies about us, when does it end? God is love. He loves us all, so we should find a way (seeking God) to love our friends and enemies. 1 Peter 3:9 says, "Do not repay evil with evil or insult with insult. On the contrary, repay evil with blessing, because to this you were called so that you may inherit a blessing."

CHAPTER 23

Have you ever wondered, if God loves me so much, then why would He want to hurt me and make me suffer? If He can stop all pain, why doesn't He do it? Thoughts can come in your head making you question God and His way of doing things. But we must lean on His word and know that His ways are not our ways. If we don't go through the afflictions, the hurt and pain, how will we be able to encourage others and our own children? As a parent, I'm sure we would like to take our kids' place when they are diagnosed with a sickness or experience a heartache. Suffering may come, but God also gives His comfort! He doesn't allow us to go through trials and tribulations just so we can struggle. He uses difficulties so we can learn from them and become wiser and more dependent on Him. Romans 8:18 says, "I consider that our present sufferings are not worth comparing with the glory that will be revealed in us."

Has there been a moment (or times) where you felt you just couldn't make it, but HOPE was the only thing that kept you going? A hope in God, even though you haven't given Him much time? A hope that He will listen and come through when you need Him the most? A hope that He will remove you from the mess you created for yourself? No matter how deep the hole is that you have dug yourself in, God can reach down and pull you out by His love and grace for each of us! Romans 5:8 says, "But God demonstrates His own love for us in this: While we were still sinners, Christ died for us."

Psalm 119:84-86 says, "How long must your servant wait? When will you punish my persecutors? The arrogant dig pits to trap me, contrary to your law. All your commands are trustworthy; help me, for I am being persecuted without cause." How many times do we feel like we are getting punished for something we didn't even do? People hate us, talk bad about us, and we wonder, "when will they get what they deserve?" No matter how the devil tries to knock you down and break you down, keep your eyes on the One who sees it all. He said He will never leave you nor forsake you. If you have nothing left to hold on to, hold on to those words "I WILL NEVER LEAVE

YOU NOR FORSAKE YOU". Psalm 33:4 says, "For the Word of the LORD is right and true; He is faithful in all He does."

Have you ever searched for someone, or something to help you remove the pain, hurt, and agony of being alone? We don't want to go through hard times. We turn to drugs, alcohol, food, or whatever we can find to numb the pain. God's words were given to us so we could experience His peace in the midst of ALL the storms we face. The more we get into His word, the more peace and joy we will experience. We will start to boldly feel this sense that "I can overcome and win this battle I'm faced with!" 2 Corinthians 1:4 says, "Who comforts us in all our troubles, so that we can comfort those in any trouble with the comfort we ourselves receive from God."

If you know Who your source is, you will never be disappointed. We may hear many things that only try to lure us from the truth. The devil never sleeps, but neither does God! Are we sharing the wisdom God gives us, or are we keeping all of our wisdom to ourselves and being foolish with it? Yes, age helps in becoming wiser; older people have seen it all, done it all; and yes, they share that with the younger generation. But you do not have to be old to be wise. God sees it all and created it all! Let's also listen to the wisdom He tells us in His word. James 3:17 says, "But the wisdom that comes from heaven is first of all pure; then peace loving, considerate, submissive, full of mercy and good fruit, impartial and sincere."

Psalm 119:113 says, "I hate double-minded people, but I love your law."

This Scripture can be hard to understand, "I hate double-minded people". God is love, so why would the word "hate" and "people" be in the same sentence? We sometimes love people but hate their sin. We must love like God does and hate what God hates. God wants us to LOVE EVERYONE! Sinners and believers, not just the ones who are "like us". God is love! We should show love, not judgment or condemnation. 1 John 2:15,16 says, "Do not love the world or anything in the world. If anyone loves the world, love for the Father is not in them. For everything in the world - the lust of the flesh, the lust of the eyes, and the pride of life - comes not from the Father but from the world."

Psalm 119:115 says, "Away from me, you evildoers, that I may keep the commands of my God!" Here is another verse that can seem confusing. We are to love people but hate their sin, but now it says, "Away from me, you evildoers"? We do not have to "hang out" with sinners to share the love of God. God knows our "flesh" is weak. Eventually, we could be tempted to do the sin they do, if we are spending too much time "hanging out". That's why we, ourselves, have to stay away from "evildoers". We don't have to "hang out" with them to show them that we love them. We are here to show God we love them, by praying for them, wishing them goodness and favor, praying God will lift them out of the pit they're in and not talking bad or judging them to other "believers". Let's build people up and build His kingdom!! 1 Corinthians 15:33 says, "Do not be misled: "Bad company corrupts good character."

CHAPTER 24

WE ALL WANT TO BE WISE. WISDOM CAN prevent us from experiencing many of the heartaches we experience. Many time's a bad behavior is what is common to us, it's our "nature". But how do we get out of that cycle that never gives us "true happiness? It can bring us temporary joy for a day, month, even a year, but we will still feel empty and alone inside. Without Him it's impossible to experience peace, joy, and true happiness. Proverbs 3:4-7 says, "Then you will win favor and a good name in the sight of God and man. Trust in the LORD with all your heart and lean not on your own understanding; In all your ways submit to him, and he will make your paths straight. Do not be wise in your own eyes; fear the LORD and shun evil."

Ecclesiastes 3:12-13 says, "I know that there is nothing better for people than to be happy and to do good while they live. That each of them may eat and drink, and find satisfaction in all their toil - this is the gift of God."

Luke 11:28 says, "He replied, "Blessed rather are those who hear the word of God and obey it."

When we feel broken and torn to pieces, we must try to remember what God tells us. He said what would happen if we disobey, but we also remember the grace and mercy given to us when we mess up time and time again. This brings us peace and the weight is lifted off of us. God knew we would mess up; but regardless of what He knows about us, that others may not know, He still chose to send His son to die for us all. Proverbs 21:2 says, "A person may think their own ways are right, but the LORD weighs the heart."

Have you ever cried yourself to sleep? Have you ever just laid there, wondering why you're going through difficulty and why heartache lingers in your mind? Have you ever prayed that the feeling would just go away? Your mind starts to drift off, looking at what others have, and you lose sight of the blessings you presently have. Ask God to remove the "selfishness" that you're feeling of wanting what others have. Ask Him to help you be grateful for what He's already given you. Romans 15:2-3 says, "Each of us should please our neighbors for their good, to build them up. For even Christ did not please Himself but, as it is written: "The insults of those who insult you have fallen on me.""

CHAPTER 25

WE ALL WANT TO BE HEARD. WE ALL WANT to voice our wants and needs to God. What about when God tells us to do something? We start to squirm and think, "There's no way I'm going to do that", but yet we want God to listen to us. Obedience is all God wants from us. If we choose "obedience" to Him over our own ways, God rejoices. Then God can start to work on us, opening doors for us to walk into new opportunities, new beginnings, and new changes. Will these "changes" all be good or comfortable? Not at all! But when we are "uncomfortable", we're growing. James 1:22 says, "Do not merely listen to the word, and so deceive yourselves. Do what it says."

Ephesians 4:29 say, "Do not let any unwholesome talk come out of your mouths, but only what is helpful for building others up according to their needs, that it may benefit those who listen."

Acts 5:39 say, "But if it is from God, you will not be able to stop these men; you will only find yourselves fighting against God."

As we get older, we learn to be more cautious about who we trust, due to betrayals and lies that we have experienced in our lives. We slowly start putting up "walls" around our heart and promise ourselves that we will protect ourselves from getting hurt again. In doing this, we do not realize that keeping our heart "sheltered" will only harden our hearts to receive true love and trust from God. We feel like we fail ourselves when we start to "let our guard down", but when we put our trust in Him, we will never be disappointed. God will never abandon you, lie to you, or manipulate you. Numbers 23:19 says, "God is not human, that he should lie, not a human being, that he should change his mind. Does he speak and then not act? Does he promise and not fulfill?"

We don't have to go around plotting or wishing bad things to happen to those who continue to do "bad" things, hurting others and getting away with it. God sees evil people, and in His timing, they will reap the consequences of their actions. Is it hoping or wishing bad on someone?

No! It's what God's word says. God will protect His people who choose to be obedient to Him, while living in a world so evil and ugly. He will take care of those accordingly, who choose to be sinful and not repent of their sins; with no regard for authority and doing as they please. Romans 12:19 says, "Do not take revenge, my dear friends, but leave room for God's wrath, for it is written: "It is mine to avenge; I will repay," says the LORD."

Why does it seem like when your enemies see you happy, they will do what they can to make you miserable? The answer can be found in John 10:10, which says, "The thief comes only to steal and kill and destroy, I have come that they may have life, and have it to the full." The enemy will use people, friends or enemies to STEAL the joy God puts in your heart, but don't run the opposite direction from God, run to Him! The devil won't get near you when you run to God. [128] Would you "bully" someone who has a bodyguard, who is tall, muscular, hoovering over someone they are protecting, or would you walk the other way in fear? That's how our Father looks like to the devil, when he tries to "bully" us (thoughts of guilt or shame). God will remove all those thoughts and give you back that peace, joy, and laughter!! Psalm 140:4 says, "Keep me safe,

LORD, from the hands of the wicked; protect me from the violent, who devise ways to trip my feet."

Hebrews 10:22 says, "Let us draw near to God with a sincere heart and with the full assurance that faith brings, having our hearts sprinkled to cleanse us from a guilty conscience and having our bodies washed with pure water."

If you are trying to build your family and your relationships on sand (hidden lies, hurts, anger, deceit, etc.), they will fall apart. We have to work on ourselves and our relationship with God in order to build a solid rock foundation. When the trials and tribulations come against your family, you will be able to withstand the storms that are meant to tear you down. Stay in the shelter of the Most High God! Isaiah 55:6 says, "Seek the LORD while he may be found; call on Him while He is near."

CHAPTER 26

IF YOU DON'T FEAR GOD, WHO WILL YOU fear? As our Father, He doesn't give us "Commandments" because He wants to withhold good things from us, or keep us from enjoying life. Being a follower of Jesus doesn't mean you will have a boring, strict, and lifeless life. No, quite the opposite! He wants you to enjoy the life He has given you with peace and joy! But He knows you won't get that if you do whatever you want to do. He gives us these "laws" to protect us from dangers, trials, tribulations, heartbreaks, and stress that lies ahead. John 15:14 says, "You are my friends if you do what I command."

Psalm 32:10 says, "Many are the woes of the wicked, but the LORD's unfailing love surrounds the one who trusts in him."

Did you receive attack after attack growing up? Can you remember all the good you did for others, yet it never seemed to matter because so many bad things still happened to you? So why give the effort to be a "good person"? Because deep down God used someone to plant that "good" seed in you. Never stop allowing people to "water" that seed that was planted when you were younger. A breakthrough is coming!! You just have to hold strong to God's promises. 2 Chronicles 16:9 says, "For the eyes of the LORD range throughout the earth to strengthen those whose hearts are fully committed to Him. You have done a foolish thing, and from now on you will be at war."

No matter how much evil people get away with, our God is righteous. He will save us from the torment that's been done to us over the years; all the disrespect, the hate, the envy...all of that will come to an end. Will people still have envy and hate in their heart? Of course. But you will now be lifted out of that pit and placed in a safe place. Galatians 5:19-21says, "The acts of the flesh are obvious: sexual immorality, impurity and debauchery; idolatry and witchcraft; hatred, discord, jealousy, fits of rage, selfish ambition, dissensions, factions and envy; drunkenness, orgies, and the like. I warn you, as I did before, that those who live like this will not inherit the kingdom of God."

We try to hide our tears, to not show others we are "weak", but inside we are screaming, crying, and asking God to help us! Crying is not a sign of weakness, but a cleansing of our souls. It's tough to go through each day carrying the burden from yesterday. We are created to be strong, but not in the sense where we feel we don't need God's help. We may not "see Him" or "feel Him", but He is ALWAYS near when we call on Him. Friends and family may have been too busy when we needed them the most, but God is never too busy for us. Deuteronomy 31:8 says, "The LORD himself goes before you and will be with you; he will never leave you nor forsake you. Do not be afraid; do not be discouraged."

CHAPTER 27

Matthew 5:22 says, "But I tell you that anyone who is angry with a brother or sister will be subject to judgment. Again, anyone who says to a brother or sister, 'Raca,' is answerable to the court. And anyone who says, 'You fool!' will be in danger of the fire of hell."

When things seem to "turn around" and good things now seem to knock at our door, we should continue to stay humble and not think "highly" of ourselves. God promises to give us prosperity and wealth, but when our hearts are ready. If He sees that giving us "success" or what we desire at the moment, will only drift us away from Him or cause us danger, He won't give it to us. Proverbs 28:26 says, "Those who trust in themselves are fools, but those who walk in wisdom are kept safe."

Deuteronomy 6:5 says, "Love the LORD your God with all your heart and with all your soul and with all your strength."

How beautiful is it to see the family of your church get along? We're all Christians trying to be loyal to the church, but are we being loyal to God outside of the church? As a church family, we have to come together, through fellowship and prayer, to be ready for the devil's schemes to bring division in a church. This can come through questions like, "Well, why are they getting more blessed than we are, they just started coming to church? Why are people not helping us when they see we have a need?" Whatever thoughts or lies the enemy tries to fill our minds with, we must remember to look to God to provide for our every need spiritually, physically, and emotionally. He is the PROVIDER of all things! Ephesians 3:20,21says, "Now to Him who is able to do immeasurably more than all we ask or imagine, according to His power that is at work within us, to Him be glory in the church and in Christ Jesus throughout all generations, for ever and ever! Amen."

Psalm 134:1 says, "Praise the LORD, all you servants of the LORD who minister by night in the house of the LORD." Servants...that can be hard to swallow. We don't want to feel "tied down" or feel like we have to "serve" anyone. We want to be able to do what we want, whenever we want. But that way of living, is living to please the flesh, which can never get enough fulfillment, or joy. We are to seek God to give us the gifts of peace and joy. We want to be servants of God, spreading His word to others!! Serving to share His love to others, helping others, and lending a hand wherever needed.

1 Peter 4:10 says, "Each of you should use whatever gift you have received to serve others, as faithful stewards of God's grace in its various forms."

Proverbs 19:17 says, "Whoever is kind to the poor lends to the LORD, and he will reward them for what they have done."

CHAPTER 28

CAN YOU IMAGINE HAVING SOMEONE LOVE you forever? A promised love that won't fade, as we change in age? A love that is given to us, when all we have to do is receive it? We don't have to jump through hoops to prove we deserve it. God has given the most precious gift to us all....Jesus Christ! The One who would come down to earth, to walk "in our shoes" and to endure the suffering we would face in our lifetime. Romans 12:9-10 says, "Love must be sincere. Hate what is evil, cling to what is good. Be devoted to one another in love. Honor one another above yourselves."

Luke 6:27 says, "But to you who are listening I say: Love your enemies, do good to those who hate you."

Psalm 91:15 says, "He will call on Me, and I will answer him; I will be with him in trouble, I will deliver him and honor him."

Matthew 15:11 says, "What goes into someone's mouth does not defile them, but what comes out of their mouth, that is what defiles them."

Does guilt seem to follow you each day as you rise in the morning? Does shame seem to follow you everywhere you go? Do you "hide" behind alcohol, drugs, food, or whatever you can find to bring you comfort? Those things will only bring you comfort and happiness for a short time. We try to find ways to escape and hide, but God still sees us. He knows your heart and wants to help you. There is no shame, guilt, or sin that can separate you from the love of God. People may "distance" themselves from you, but God is close to you. James 1:5 says, "If any of you lacks wisdom, you should ask God, who gives generously to all without finding fault, and it will be given to you."

2 Thessalonians 1:6,7 says, "God is just: He will pay back trouble to those who trouble you. 7 and give relief to you who are troubled, and to us as well. This will happen

when the LORD Jesus is revealed from heaven in blazing fire with his powerful angels."

Do you know someone who is always waging war with you? Someone who seems to always find something to pick a fight with you about? It seems like all those attacks push you back into a corner, leaving you feeling helpless and exhausted. We pray and pray and it seems like the torment keeps coming, and we can't figure out why because we've been nothing but good. You don't deserve that kind of treatment. But when you're faced with attack after attack, it's because the devil knows God has an important assignment for you. He will use anyone to torment you, to make you stumble and give up on the plan God has set out for you. Romans 8:28 says, "And we know that in all things God works for the good of those who love Him who have been called according to His purpose."

Do you feel like people always want to see you fail? Do you wonder why people can't be happy for you? We are all given an opportunity to do something great with our life, but sometimes the setbacks we face in life prolong where we thought we would be by now. Loss of a loved one, loss of a job or home, and many other hardships may come against you, but keep pressing forward, knowing you don't have to do it alone. God will lift you up and walk with you through the hardships you face. Deuteronomy 31:8 says, "The LORD himself goes before you and will be with you; he will never leave you nor forsake you. Do not be afraid; do not be discouraged."

Many time's we find ourselves cornered and defeated. Many time's the battles we face are not against people, but against depression, loneliness, anger, bitterness, or jealousy. We don't feel worthy. The friends who we thought were friends, left us in our time of need. So now we're left alone to fight these "emotions" on our own. Ephesians 6:12 says, "For our struggle is not against flesh and blood, but against the rulers, against the authorities, against the powers of this dark world and against the spiritual forces of evil in the heavenly realms."

It may seem at times that God has left us. We wonder why He's allowing us to suffer and why there is so much evil in the world. Isn't God love? Doesn't He protect His children? We may find ourselves questioning God; but what the enemy meant for evil, God will use for good. Temptation may come, for us to get angry with God for "not helping" in our time of need, or for removing someone we love so much. But God knows the future. He knows what tomorrow holds. He knows who's going to be walking your journey with you and who needs to be put in your path to complete the purpose He has for you. Proverbs 19:21 says, "Many are the plans in a person's heart, but it is the LORD's purpose that prevails."

Titus 2:11,12 says, "For the grace of God has appeared that offers salvation to all people. 12 It teaches us to say "No" to ungodliness and worldly passions, and to live self-controlled, upright and godly lives in this present age."

Are we looking to others to encourage us? Are we waiting and seeking guidance from others on what we should do? What happens when the day comes that their life gets too busy to "encourage" you or tell you what they think you should do? Life changes. Life can get so "fast-paced" that in the blink of an eye, your kids have grown up and left the house. You're left alone. Left seeking and wondering, "What is my purpose now?" We all have a purpose in life and if we can go out and help others, we will see the shift in how valuable we are and how there are people out there wanting a friend. Someone needs you! Ephesians 2:10

says, "For we are God's handiwork, created in Christ Jesus to do good works, which God prepared in advance for us to do."

If you think you're alone in the world, you're not. Your spouse may have left you; you may have had parents say you will never amount to anything. You may have heard that no one would ever want you. God wants you! God loves you! God has great things in store for you. He created you and He know's the potential you have hidden inside of you. You are a child of the Most High God, your Father is a King!! How amazing is that? God not only wants you to know about Him, but He wants to have a relationship with you, to be your friend, to be the One you run to, the One you tell all your problems to. Proverbs 27:5-6 says, "Better is open rebuke than hidden love. Wounds from a friend can be trusted, but an enemy multiplies kisses."

John 16:33 says, "I have told you these things, so that in me you may have peace. In this world you will have trouble. But take heart! I have overcome the world."

Psalm 147:10,11 says, "His pleasure is not in the strength of the horse, nor his delight in the legs of the warrior; the LORD delights in those who fear him, who put their hope in his unfailing love." God is not worried about how much money you make. God is not impressed with how your attendance is at church. What God wants, is for you to FEAR Him. He wants us to have that "loving" fear that causes us to be obedient to our Father. He knows what's best for us. I'm sure we've all heard our parents tell us, "I only tell you this because I love you; I discipline you because I love you and don't want you to make the same mistakes I did". Well God endured everything we are suffering now. He tells us in the Bible what to do when trials and temptations come our way because He loves us. He wants to protect us; He cares for us.

2 Thessalonians 3:3 says, "But the LORD is faithful, and He will strengthen you and protect you from the evil one."

CHAPTER 29

NO MATTER WHAT STORM WE'RE IN RIGHT now, we must praise God that He is going to bring us through. We aren't the first to experience a loss of a loved one, a broken heart, or financial struggles. And look just how God has gotten others through their storms. If it weren't for the struggles, we wouldn't always be able to see how good God really is. What the devil meant for evil, God will use it for good. Keep pressing forward even when it seems like the forces on the other side are too strong for you to handle. God is on your side! He will hold back those coming against you. Proverbs 16:7 says, "When the LORD takes pleasure in anyone's way, he causes their enemies to make peace with them."

Do you ever look at the sunset and just think, "Wow, that is God!?" Do you ever stop to wake up early enough to just sit outside and see the sunrise? Do you think of what a blessing it is to be here another day and just to acknowledge God and His creation of Heaven and Earth? We don't always look to acknowledge the little things in life until life forces us to do so .When we see life from a different perspective, from a hospital bed, or from an abandonment, from a divorce, or whatever tragedy has happened, let's be reminded of the One who loves us and wants us to return to Him in our times of despair and hurt. Life is beautiful, and we must love the Creator, our Father in Heaven, who made such beautiful things! The devil hates a thankful heart because it helps us overcome life's struggles. 1 Corinthians 15:57 says, "But thanks be to God! He gives us the victory through our LORD Jesus Christ."

Psalm 149:1 says, "Sing to the LORD a new song, His praise in the assembly of His faithful people." Sometimes we need to change the "station" as far as what we speak. It's the same old song that is being played on replay. We talk about the person we loved and who did us wrong or we talk about the aches in our body to anyone who asks and will listen. Whenever we change those thoughts in our heads, that person no longer has a hold on us. If the one you loved left you, that doesn't mean you're not lovable, it may mean that in the season you're in, that person wasn't going to help you fulfill the purpose God has for you, and if it's God's will, He will bring that person back as a changed person! [129] God is an All-Knowing, All-Powerful, loving Father.

CONCLUSION

IN LIFE, WE WILL WALK THROUGH MANY valleys and experience many mountaintops. There will be hard times where we feel like quitting. There will be moments where we feel like we are cornered with no way of escape. But through those hardships, we come out refined and pure; pure from all the emotions that hit us like a tidal wave. Purified from fear, loneliness, betrayal, depression, feeling lost, tiredness, weakness, and feeling unimportant. So many emotions! Emotions that appear to be more pain than pleasure, more sadness than joy. We wonder when we are going to get that "breakthrough" that we keep hearing about. It always seems like we're competing for someone's approval, looking for love, or competing for a love that was never present.

So now in life we are filled with doubt and sorrow. We wonder if we are worthy to be loved. You may feel like no one understands how you feel or what you've been through. But God saw you all along...the suffering, the criticism, the lies, the persecution, the slander, the insults, the troubles, and the verbal cruelty. He saw it all! Why didn't God rescue me from all the heartaches, the sufferings, the hardships, and all the tears shed? Because God knows what you were equipped with. He created you. He wanted to put you through fire to bring you out refined, stronger, wiser, and pure! Like gold has to be put through fire to become something beautiful, He had to break you, shake you, and mold you into the masterpiece He designed you to be. You had to bring that beauty within to the surface! He wanted you to see you had far more worth than what the world called you. The world called you orphan, helpless, unlovable, ugly, and dumb. No matter what bricks were thrown at you, He was using those bricks to build a barrier around you.

You wonder what you could have done differently to make them love you, what you could have compromised to make them stay. As the years pass by, little by little, we compromise, we lose ourselves, and we lose our identity seeking others to make us happy, or we are too busy pleasing others, to make them happy, that we don't care to make ourselves happy.

God's given each one of us a purpose in life. We all have different roles to play in this world. We should encourage one another, lift a fellow person when we see them fallen, lift the spirits of others, and not laugh at pains and failures. Many times, all we want is to be accepted, to feel like we fit in somewhere. We beat ourselves up, questioning, reasoning, and wanting answers that no man can give. No man or woman can give you the love that they never really received as a child growing up. The "love" they received was given with conditions. We can't look to others to show us or give us love, when they never really received it growing up. They can't give you something they don't have. Through the book of Psalms, we read about so many things that we feel - past, present, and future.

Disappointments and heartbreaks are inevitable and unavoidable. But the solution is not! God is the same yesterday, today, and tomorrow! Hebrews 13:8 tells us that there's nothing we go through that is a surprise to Jesus. He knew the dangers we would face. He knew the persecution and the hate we would endure. He knows we are weak, easily tempted, and foolish.

Despite all the imperfections in us, He still chose to carry that cross, that cross where He would lay down His life for us. I know it would be hard to give up one of our beloved children for a crime someone else committed. Jesus paid the ultimate price for sins He knew we would commit. John 3:16 tells us that God sent His One and only Son to be a sacrifice for each of us!

We all want to be happy, we all want peace, and we all want to live that "happy ever after" life. However, life is not a fairytale. To live that happily ever after life, we have to seek the One who can give us joy forever! The more we seek God the more He starts to fill our hearts with His presence. Those past hurts, the pains of betrayal, the insecurities, and the insults that you've stored in your heart will start to melt away. When you want to take out those past memories and dwell on them, remind yourself that Jesus has taken all the hurts, all the pain, all the unforgiveness and replaced it with a peace and joy that surpasses all things!

There's no room for us to serve two masters...God and the devil. We want God when we want healing, justice, miracles, money, protection, and rest. And we want the devilish things when we want to "have fun", live reckless, and please our flesh with partying, drunkenness, lust of the eyes, greed, and selfishness. 1 Peter 5:8 says, "Be alert and of sober mind. Your enemy the devil prowls around like a roaring lion looking for someone to devour." The things of the flesh will never bring us true peace and joy. All the "worldly" things will not fill the void we have in our heart, the void of having a parent abandon you, the void of a loved one dying, or the void of a person you loved now telling you they no longer love you and walking away from a relationship you had so much invested in. You are now left alone, abandoned, and feeling like you serve no purpose. Who are you to care for? Who are you to share your love with? You wonder who could want you all broken, torn apart, and you feel like "used goods", but God will always want you! He wants to be invited into your heart, to start to reconstruct what the enemy stole and broke. He wants to make you whole again!! God is a God of restoration!! You will love again. You will smile again. You will trust again. You will be made whole again!

That's His promise for you. He doesn't break promises; He's not one to lie.

The more you fellowship with God, the more He will reveal to you why you went through the struggles, the hardships, and the trials that seemed to just come against you back to back. God will give you PROVISION (providing something for use) and more DISCERNMENT (the ability to judge well). You walked through life "blind", blind to people's intentions towards you and blind to being deceived because you saw the goodness in everyone and everything. Your eyes will open, to see clearly how many people walk around with hurt in their hearts, hurting others.

God loves us just the way we are. He wants us, when others make us feel unlovable and uncared for. He wants to adopt each of us into His family, which is the family of believers, that knows how to love, show compassion, forgive, and keep lifting each other up and giving a hand to someone who's fallen. Curious, tired, exhausted of the life you're living? If you don't know someone who you can call that will pray with you, get on your knees and pray and cry out to God! He is listening! If you believe that Jesus Christ died on the cross for you and three days later, rose from the dead, that He loves you, that even when it seems like you have nothing to offer him, He will welcome you with open arms. You can unpack all your "baggage" there, and walk in the freedom Jesus died for you to have. Matthew 11:28-30 says, "Come to me, all you who are weary and burdened, and I will give you rest. Take my yoke upon you and learn from me, for I am gentle and humble in heart, and you will find rest for your souls. For my yoke is easy and my burden is light."

Continue to seek the help your soul desires. Continue to seek God asking Him reveal to you the areas in your life that need to "be fixed" and the areas in your life that need to be healed. Keep your eyes on God, the One who can rescue you and lift you out of the pit you have dug yourself in. Remember I love you and God loves you! God Bless, stay blessed, and look to be a blessing to others!

[11]This needs to be explained more. Readers unfamiliar with evil spirits will struggle to make the connection without further explanation.

[12]What does this mean? How does God "go to work on us". Add some details about what that may look like or feel like.

[13]Use a different description. Readers do not want to have it in their minds that what they are reading will be repetitive. Say something like "you may hear concepts or principles discussed more than once.

[14]Based on how you change the word the first time make a change here. Maybe to "God will put things in our hearts multiple time"

[15]This statement needs some clarification. Though you mention your ex-husband in the dedication, this is the first time he is brought up.

[I6]Give more scriptural context for this so readers know "what" does not count against them.

[I7]

[I8]Leave out specific places so the each reader can relate.

[I9]Explain what the narrow path means

[I10]Explain this better…some people seek God but still feel hurt so maybe explain on a spiritual level how He does this even though we may still feel hurt (emotions)

[I11]Do you have a scripture you can use to back up this statement?

[I12]Do you mean physically walk with us…clarify

[I13]Clarify this statement…maybe change "serving" to "giving into" or "falling prey to"

[I14]Are you intending for these verses to apply the paragraph above or below? They do not seem to tie into either. You will need to write a tie in.

[115]Do you have a scripture you can put here that speaks to being grateful?

[116]Add more of this verse for context.

[117]I think this needs further clarification. Maybe say "in a marriage, a spouse is protective of the love relationship and desires to fix anything that breaks it or threatens to hurt it. In the same way, God is protective of the love relationship He has with us and rises up against anything that would threaten it. This is the type of jealousy God has for us. This is different than unhealthy jealousy born out of insecurity."

[118]This needs a quick tie in to the above paragraph and should be part of the paragraph.

[119]Explain this statement more so the reader understands what it means that we all have "demons". Do you mean actual demons or struggles and strongholds?

[120]I don't think this statement is needed.

[121]Something needs to be added to the end of this paragraph that ties the verse into what happiness in God is.. peace, companionship, knowing our Creator...these are all concepts found in the scripture you use.

[122]This statement makes it seem like the other words of the Bible are not as important. If you want to keep this statement, explain that the words in Red are the words of Jesus and why they are significant but do this without reducing the importance of the other words.

[123]Preface this with a scripture about fearing the Lord.

[124]This needs an explanation tied into the first sentence. Explain how others are waiting to hear the goodness of God as a testimony so we should speak God's truth instead of gossip or drama.

[125]I would change this to sought by us.

[126]Needs to be reworded. This makes it seem like God's feelings about us are based on our actions and that His feelings change as our actions change.

[127]It is unclear what you are trying to say here.

[128]This needs to be reworded.

[129]This is not the only reason that God removes people from our lives. Consider revising this statement.